THE PSALMS

*It is
you alone
who are
my hope...*

THE PSALMS

Meditations for Every Day of the Year

JOAN D. CHITTISTER, OSB

A Crossroad Book
The Crossroad Publishing Company
New York

1996

The Crossroad Publishing Company
370 Lexington Avenue, New York, NY 10017

Copyright © 1996 by Joan D. Chittister, OSB

Title page art by Jeffry A. Braun

Printed in the United States of America

Library of Congress Cataloging-in-Publication Data

Chittister, Joan.
    The Psalms : meditations for every day of the year / Joan D.
Chittister.
    p. cm.
    ISBN 0-8245-1581-1 (pbk.)
    1. Bible. O.T. Psalms–Meditations. 2. Devotional calendars.
I. Title.
BS1430.4.C48 1996
242'.2–dc20   96-13864
                                              CIP

This book is dedicated to Mary Grace Hanes, OSB,
who gives without counting hours,
and because of whose unfailing support
and flawless service
more good things have been accomplished
than time could ever allow.

INTRODUCTION

The psalms are the oldest prayers in the Judeo–Christian tradition. There are 150 of them and, like hymns today, they were written for multiple occasions. They are a lexicon of the human condition. They trace the human condition back thousands of years. They assure us that our own hopes and fears, desires and emotions are just like the rest of the human condition. Say each month's verse from the psalms before every reading. By the end of the month, say it from memory. It will find a soft spot in your heart. Most of all, it will bring your heart the comfort of the ages.

JANUARY

Psalm 42

*Like the deer longs
for running waters,
so my soul longs
for you, O God.
Athirst is my soul
for God, the living God.
When shall I go
and behold the face of God?*

Longing, you see, is part of life. The only question is, what do you long for? Don't be glib about the answer. Look down deep inside yourself. What is lacking when you feel empty? What are you really thinking about when you're supposed to be thinking about something else? That's what you're longing for. Find it. It's the key to your problems in the present and the energy you have for the future.

Nobody is ever completely happy, completely satisfied. That's not because we're failures. That's because we're built that way. We're supposed to want more — or why would we ever want God enough to go through life with a restless eye, watching. Be grateful for your longings. They are what take us to the next step in life and there are many to be walked before we're whole, before we're finally home.

Someplace along the way in life we all need to learn to long for God, for what really counts. The hard thing, the good thing, is that life itself will teach us that.

January 1: What we long for is what we are. What we long for describes both our values and our needs. If we long for love, for instance, we may value peace at any price. We may need approval. If we long for attention, we may value crises. We may need turmoil around us in order to satisfy our own desire to be seen as the savior of the family or the parish or the community. The psalmist longs for God. And what are the implications of that?

January 2: For what do you long? No, not what do you "want." What do you "long for" when your heart aches or the work fails or the week is busy? Look underneath the particular situation and find the reason for the longing. What is that saying to you about the purpose of your life?

January 3: It is so easy to go through life half alive and never even know it. Pretty soon we get used to the dullness inside of us, to the fact that nothing gives us energy anymore, that nothing excites us, that nothing really matters in life but getting one thing done and going on to the next. Life becomes an exercise in plodding instead of living. But the psalmist longs for God so much that God is a human distraction, day in and day out. What do you think about when you should be thinking about something else? What is that telling you?

January 4: A soul that longs for something is a soul that is growing — one way or another, smaller or larger. What have your longings done to your life and its horizons — broadened them or crippled them?

January 5: Don't be afraid of whatever it is that you long to have. Until you face the longing that is consuming you, you can't work it through. Until you accept it, you can't deal with it. Whatever we long for has growth in it for us. Think of something you have longed for in life. What did you get in life as a result of that longing — whether you ever got the particular thing you wanted or not?

January 6: To long for God is to center our lives on what we cannot see. How beautiful! After all, everything we can see never satisfies us completely. So life must really be somewhere else, right?

January 7: Longing is such a wonderful thing. It tells us that we're not finished yet. Those who long for nothing are already half dead.

January 8: An epiphany is any moment in time that leads us to a new insight about life in general. A graduation, for instance, may bring us to a new understanding about our social responsibility to the world at large. When we find ourselves longing for God more than we do for lesser things, we are living in a state of epiphany. All of life takes on a different glow; nothing is small anymore, nothing is useless. Only God, you see, really gives life meaning.

January 9: We spend so much time wanting what we do not have. Be careful that your longings don't erase today. Name two good things that happened to you this morning. Remember that happiness is not a period of time in anybody's life. It is a different moment every day.

January 10: Longing is a compass that guides us through life. We may never get what we really want, that's true, but every step along the way will be determined by it. So, when something goes wrong, it isn't so much what we did that's wrong; it's what we wanted so badly that we went the wrong way to get it that is in question. What do you want in life right now? What kinds of things are you doing as a result of it? Is it bringing the best out of you? Be honest.

January 11: Joseph Campbell wrote: "We must be willing to get rid of the life we've planned, so as to have the life that is waiting for us. The old skin has to be shed before the new one can come." Sometimes our longings make it impossible for us to live the life in front of us. It's so easy to want what we don't have and miss what we do have.

January 12: Life is a series of resurrections, provided we're willing to let old things die. What little deaths have you been through that have already enabled new life, new longings in you?

January 13: The great Chinese philosopher Lau Tzu wrote: *Great trouble comes / from not knowing what is enough. / Great conflict arises from wanting too much. / When we know when enough is enough, / There will always be enough.* It is one thing to long for something; it is another to be at its mercy.

January 14: The traveler asked, "What kind of weather are we going to have today?" And the old shepherd said, "The kind of weather I like." "How do you know it will be the kind of weather you like?" the traveler scoffed. "Having found out, sir, I cannot always get what I like, I have learned always to like what I get. So I am quite sure we will have the kind of weather I like." Life is good. It's not necessary to long for another. But, oh, it takes so long to learn that.

January 15: Today is the birthday of Martin Luther King, Jr., a man who longed for the reign of God with profound discontent. Imagine what the world could be like if you and I could do the same. Maybe longing for God is the dis-ease the world really needs. Maybe it is what is really missing in us — the thing that makes the difference between spirituality and religion.

January 16: Here's the happy by-product of longing for God: it saves us from lesser longings. Have you learned to long for God yet, or are you still stuck at another level? That's all right; you'll learn. Trust your dissatisfactions.

January 17: The Sufi proverb teaches, "There would not be such a thing as counterfeit gold if there were no real gold somewhere." Isn't that a fact? There is so much in life that is illusory: we assume that marrying someone will assure happiness; that one person can satisfy all our needs; that achievement will assure us of friends; that money provides what we need.

We spend years chasing plastic rainbows. Maybe that's why life is often so hard. We keep bumping our noses on our own bad choices and false expectations.

January 18: "Three feet of ice are not frozen in one day," the Chinese say. What is worth having in life takes time to achieve. God is a lifelong process that winds through trial and error, failure and tiny triumphs. It is not an exercise in quick fixes.

January 19: Beware what drives you on. "If you would be pope, you can think of nothing else," the Spanish proverb teaches. What we long for regulates our actions, shapes our motives, determines our relationships, directs our hearts, consumes our lives. What is it that consumes yours? What would the psalmist say about that?

January 20: January is a month famous for its founders of religious communities: Elizabeth Ann Seton and the Sisters of Charity; Francis de Sales and Jane Frances de Chantal, the Visitations; Angela Merici, the Ursulines; John Bosco, the Salesians. These people all longed for the reign of God on earth and mobilized others to work for it in intense and concentrated ways. The question is, what great life-longing for others have I mobilized to effect? To what groups do I belong and work for that bring good for others?

January 21: "Like the deer longs for running waters" — like a natural passion, an uncontrollable urge, like a physical need, the psalmist wants God. Now that is big stuff. For most of us, for most of our lives, God is a yawn and a ritual. For people who know how short life really is, for those who expect fewer new years in the future than they have had in the past, God — the uncomfortable awareness of the Beyond — begins to be a passion, an urge, a physical process. And in what stage of life are you: yawning or thirsting?

January 22: "When? When!" the psalmist demands. When will all my wants be fulfilled? Or when will I sink into God? The first demand can't happen here. The second can.

January 23: "Life is like a jig-saw puzzle," the wag wrote, "with some of the pieces missing." And that's the key to life right there. Notice that the psalmist talks about the "soul" longing for God. It is the deep-down part of us, in other words, that comes to realize that there is, indeed, a piece missing. Don't rush to fill it. A little emptiness is good for the human heart.

January 24: If God is still a cardboard cutout in your life — still remote, still unknown, still impersonal — you haven't spent nearly enough time walking in the country, sitting in the dark, or laughing with friends. How can you be thirsty for what you have never tasted?

January 25: Name three people you know. Which one of them speaks to you best of longing for God? What tells you that? Be careful on this one. Remember that we have little evidence that Jesus spent a lot of time in church.

January 26: The psalmist is wailing about finding God someplace else. Don't be fooled by that. God is right here. "Put God into your life," the preacher harangued. "Ah," the mystic said, "How sad! The fact is that God is already in our lives. All we really have to do is learn to recognize that."

January 27: Name three things you're going to do today. Which one of them reflects what you long for in life? Now, how far away from real life is it?

January 28: "When shall I go and behold the face of God?" the psalmist wonders out loud. "When shall I die?" he asks himself. How much time do you spend thinking about death? What effect does it have on you? Now, think: how much time do you spend thinking about "beholding the face of God"? They're two different things, you know. The one is a natural process. The other we can do ourselves. Now there's a thought.

January 29: "Those who wish to sing always find a song," the Swedish proverb says. We get what we long for, in other words. I had a friend who used to warn us, "Watch how you word your prayers, because you're going to get what you want." Have you ever gotten what you wanted only to wish you had never gotten it at all? And what did you learn from that?

January 30: Bernadette Devlin wrote, "To gain that which is worth having, it may be necessary to lose everything else." Do you want anything enough to give up everything else in your life, if necessary, to get it? If you don't, you have my sympathy.

January 31: "On the Plains of Hesitation," wrote George W. Cecil, "bleach the bones of countless millions who, at the Dawn of Victory, sat down to wait, and waiting — died." Want something, anything, bad enough to do something to get it. It may not be the best thing you could have wanted, but you will soon find that out. Then, when you realize that you must change, you will know how important to life, to survival, to happiness, longing really is.

FEBRUARY

PSALM 103

*God touches all
in the heavens
and on earth.
Everything is full
of sacred presence.*

*I*f life is anything at all, it is, for most of us most of the time, dullness punctuated by the unpredictable. For the most part, we get up day after day, month after month, year after year to do the same things over and over again. Take out the garbage. Do the wash. Attend the meetings. Fill out the forms. Get the job done. Go shopping. Make the telephone calls. Do the dishes. Visit the relatives. Meet the deadlines. Over and over and over again we grind our way through one year after another: holding the fort; running the line; keeping the faith. Dull. Boring. Beautiful.

One of life's best — and slowest — lessons is that it is in ordinariness where God waits for us. It is in the ordinary that we too often miss the Sacred Presence. So inured are we to life around us that we don't even see it anymore. While we touch the holy in our very hands we look for it elsewhere.

We want life to be exciting, when, as a matter of fact, life is only life. We want the spiritual to be mystical rather than real. We want to be something we aren't and when that doesn't happen we want to be left alone to decay in the humdrum, sure that life has passed us by.

What we need to come to understand is that what is real for us is the only piece of the sacred we can be sure of in life. After all, where else can we find God except where we are?

February 1: Lots of things that are ordinary we do not want to accept. Misunderstandings, for instance, are quite common. But we fall apart when they happen and brood for days and think about them months later. Families fall apart because of misunderstandings and good works are sabotaged everywhere as a result of them. But with goodwill on both parts — the will, that is, to hear the other's concern and respond to it — a misunderstanding is only a misunderstanding. An ordinary, garden-variety type of misunderstanding. Not a calamity. Not the end of the world. Just an ordinary call to do some extraordinary listening. The next time you find yourself in the middle of a misunderstanding say, "Let's go through this thing again. Only this time I'll say what you want me to hear and you say what I want you to hear." It can make an ordinary difficulty a lot of fun. Try it.

February 2: An ordinary day is a day when nothing goes the way you thought it would. That's God trying to get your attention. Think of yesterday, for instance. What didn't go as you expected it would? What was the point of the message?

February 3: The need for excitement is an addiction. It's plain old ordinary time that really makes life rich. What's the dullest thing you will do today? Tell yourself what's good about it — like: it keeps me indoors and out of the weather; it gives me some time to be alone; it gives me time to get to know the kids by asking them personal questions — and then enjoy it mightily.

February 4: There's no doubt about it: too much chocolate can kill a taste for chocolate. What are you doing so much of now that, though it's good for you, you have come to dislike it deeply? The solution is easy. Either do less of it or more of something else that gives you joy. Me, I keep trying new computer programs. And what do you do to take the edge off doing the dull stuff?

February 5: Just because a thing is ordinary does not make it useless. It may simply make it obscure. A riot of roses in springtime is ordinary but missed by many. A bank of snow in February is ordinary and ignored by most. Look at something in your home, your office, your neighborhood today that you've seen for years. What's wonderful, beautiful, soulful about it that you haven't noticed in it before?

February 6: "Don't do things to not die, do things to enjoy living," Bernie Siegel wrote. All the vitamins in the world won't do a thing for our quality of life unless we add a little love, a day of fishing, and a moment of velvet silence to our days.

February 7: The thing that's hard to believe when we say Psalm 103 is that everything, everything, is full of sacred presence. What is it in your life that you like least now? What's the sacred presence in that? See? It's in everything. Say the versicle again. And smile.

February 8: Everything around us looks pathetically ordinary until we understand its place in our lives. The dog, the old easy chair, the pictures on the wall, the desk, the woman next door are all telling us something about ourselves. Look again. Once you understand them you will never see them the same way again.

February 9: Ordinariness is not about boredom. Ordinariness is about choice. What ordinary thing will you choose to make pleasant today? How?

February 10: Today is the feast of St. Scholastica, the twin sister of St. Benedict and foundress of the first communities of Benedictine women. She was an ordinary person, apparently. No miracles are attributed to her name. No great human achievements are recorded of her. But she has never been forgotten because she took her ordinary life and lived it well. What will people say about you and your capacity for the ordinary?

February 11: Don't confuse things. International travel can get to be very ordinary. National summits can bore a person to tears. Nothing, in other words, is inherently stimulating. It all depends on the meaning beyond the meaning that we attach to them. For some people, gardening is a task. For others, it is participation in creation. So what's boring you? What you ordinarily do or what you ordinarily think?

February 12: "I love you" are the three most ordinary words in the world. I have never heard of one person who is bored by them. Explain that.

February 13: Here's a thought: everything I do today carries within it a flash of the divine. All I have to do to get it is to notice it as it whizzes by. (Sorry. Not original. The psalmist got there before me ages ago. I guess some people have realized the power of the ordinary for a long, long time.)

February 14: This is a great month for ordinary people — St. Blase, St. Valentine, St. Thomas More, Frederick Chopin, Charles Dickens, Babe Ruth, Abraham Lincoln, Susan B. Anthony. They were all types who simply did what was in front of them to do. What's in front of you that you know you should do but don't? You're still looking for someone unusual or something spectacular to do it instead, huh? No wonder too little gets done in life.

February 15: "There is no cure for birth and death," George Santayana wrote, "save to enjoy the interval." If you're not, you should be. Why do you refuse?

February 16: If I cook dinner, that's ordinary. If I put a flower on the table when I serve it, that's divine. Do something divine for someone this week.

February 17: "The tragedy of life," wrote Albert Schweitzer, "is what dies inside a person while they live." What is most alive in you right now? Joy? Awe? Contentment? Satisfaction? What have you allowed to die in yourself? Run — do not walk — to your nearest friend. Tell them what it is and ask them to help you get it back.

February 18: When today is over, ask yourself what extraordinary feeling, insight, idea came to you while you were doing the most ordinary of things. Give thanks for that. Don't forget.

February 19: The function of routine is to give us time to recoup our energies for the next unpredictable challenge. Enjoy every minute of normal time you have. Store it in your heart as energy and endurance. You will someday need the peace and calm and certainty you have garnered there.

February 20: I saw an ad today for new bullets that penetrate bulletproof vests and slice organs with "razor-like projectiles." It's a sad moment in the development of the human race — so far unfinished — when violence is more ordinary than trust. Go ahead, risk it. Talk to a stranger. Nicely. Hold the deterioration of this violent country at bay for one second longer than now seems likely.

February 21: "To live," Antoine de Saint-Exupéry wrote, "is to be slowly born." The fact is that coming to be fully alive is the task of a lifetime. There's so much in each of us that we have never touched, so much beauty we're steeped in that we've overlooked.

Today look at someone around you and tell yourself what you like about that person. Consciousness is what lifts the ordinary to the level of the sublime.

February 22: Life, by definition, is warm and pulsating. Life, by definition, speaks of God. Unawareness of those things is not ordinary; it is pathological. Where is God in your life right now? Now.

February 23: Waiting for the next world, using the next world as an excuse to ignore this one, mocks the ordinary presence of God in life. Make this world the best it can be. Start where you are. Today.

February 24: Name three ordinary things you are accustomed to doing every single day. What does each of them say to you about the presence of God in your life?

February 25: "In three words I can sum up everything I've learned about life," Robert Frost said. "It goes on." The important thing is that as life goes on so do we — that we go on enjoying it, that we go on learning from it, that we go on planning for the future. Otherwise, our ordinary lives will become a living death long before death is decent enough to come.

February 26: Of course the ordinary parts of life can feel dull sometimes. Thank God for dullness. It gives us the opportunity to appreciate what isn't. The only danger in dullness comes from finding it preferable to the provocation of possibility.

February 27: Never shrink from the ordinary. Simply ask what is in it that you have not seen before? What lesson lies in wait for you there?

February 28: I work at an ordinary desk; I live in an ordinary house; I drive a very ordinary car; I like ordinary food. The blessing of ordinariness is that it keeps me in touch with the rest of the human race and very, very interested in the extraordinary sacredness of the universe that is so unlike me, so inviting. Dag Hammarskjöld called it "the holiness of human life, before which we bow down in worship."

MARCH

PSALM 30

*You changed
my mourning
into dancing;
you removed
my sackcloth
and clothed me
with joy.*

It is interesting how we search for joy and despise suffering. Yet, suffering is a natural part of life with much to teach us and much to give us. Suffering gives us freedom and new opportunities. Joy gives us respite on the long road of life and an appreciation for heart-stopping beauty in the midst of the mundane. Most important of all, however, is the fact that suffering and joy come from the same place. Whatever is giving you your greatest happiness right now is the only thing that can really cause you great pain. Whatever is causing your suffering right now is the place beyond which you must now move in order to be able to live life joyfully again. Suffering and joy move us from end point to end point in life. They are the finger of God beckoning us to grow beyond where we are right now so that new and wonderful things can happen to us again, still, yet.

March 1: Suffering is one of the very few things in life that can only be appreciated once it is over. To have someone tell you to count your blessings when whatever blessings you remember seem so remote is itself a special kind of cruelty. On those days, there is nothing left to do but to go on in sheer faith, in rugged good will, in steady character and without whining. Perhaps you will be surprised to find out that there is a sense of relief and achievement in that alone.

March 2: If suffering is itself a good, is it holy to seek it? Definitely not. People who like to suffer, who intend to suffer, who relish suffering have another suffering and it is not suffering. No, suffering is not to be sought. It is simply to be faced so that life can become better again. It is simply to be coped with in ways that are positive so that new things can begin in life.

March 3: Suffering proves the resilience of the human spirit. Once we have known loss, there is no joy of which we are not capable.

March 4: Would life be a better place without suffering? Not necessarily. Can you imagine a party that never ends? Come on, now, confess: how long could you really take "all those wonderful people" without some time alone to balance the noise? That's what life without suffering would be like — one long stream of unappreciated events. Now there's a thought.

March 5: The beauty of suffering is that it enables us to understand the suffering of others.

March 6: Suffering is what tempers the arrogance of youth and turns us into men and women who finally know that to be finite, to be vulnerable, to be weak is not to be a failure. It is to be human.

March 7: Without suffering it is questionable whether or not we would ever come to know God. After all, who would need God?

March 8: The one time in life when we are thrown back completely on our own resources comes when we suffer. If there is nothing inside of us to enable that — no willingness to wait, no tolerance for the unknown, no inner reservoir of strength, no character for new beginnings, no spiritual life — then yes, suffering will defeat us, not because it is stronger than we are, but because we have failed to be as strong as it is.

March 9: The real problem with suffering lies not in the pain itself, but in the temptation to dull it with anything at hand — with drugs, with alcohol, with money, with noise, with activity. The purpose of life is to come to peace within ourselves. Then suffering can hardly touch us.

March 10: There are enough sufferings in life without creating them. The world will not end if the potatoes are done before the meat or the car stalls at traffic lights or the maintenance man doesn't call back or the computer keeps hanging up. The world will pinch at times like that, yes, but it will not end. Why waste all that energy acting as if it has?

March 11: When suffering comes, as suffering surely will, take a deep breath and concentrate on doing something good for yourself. Walk on the beach, begin the enrichment program you've always wanted to take, go away for a weekend, go visit a friend. Pamper yourself somehow. Pampering is the way we remind ourselves in dark times that there are still wee, bright lights in the world, even in our sere one.

March 12: A Spanish proverb reads: "From a fallen tree, all make kindling." Good comes out of everything eventually, in other words. Think for a minute: what could not have happened in your life if this suffering had not come? Sometimes it's someone we meet; sometimes it's something new we do. But it's always, always something.

March 13: "A wounded deer leaps highest," the poet Emily Dickinson wrote. And isn't it true? It's the obstacles we have to transcend in life that bring out the best in us.

March 14: Helen Keller wrote: "Although the world is full of suffering, it is full also of the overcoming of it." And Helen Keller, the deaf and blind woman who brought human communication to others like herself and changed the world for the deaf and blind ever since, ought to know.

March 15: Nothing can destroy us unless we ourselves permit it to take us down. My motto will never show up in marble but it works for me: just keep putting one foot in front of the other.

March 16: Here's the interesting, the tough, the beautiful truth: joy and sorrow come from the same place. It is only what we love, in other words, that can really make us suffer. So if you want to know from where your hard spots in life will come, just ask yourself what you really love the most. Be honest: *really* love. It's there in that place alone where loss and lesson wait.

March 17: "We can't rid the world of sorrow, but we can choose to live in joy," the Bhagavad Gita teaches. But that is the spiritual lesson that finally changes all of life. I used to be a miserable feminist, for instance, before I realized that no little patriarchal system in the world could make me unhappy. Then I learned life's real lesson: joy frees. Joy makes a person dangerous.

March 18: James Oppenheim wrote: "The foolish seek happiness in the distance, the wise grow it under their feet." Who have you made happy today while you were sitting around waiting for somebody to make you happy?

March 19: It's not easy to be happy. When you're happy you have to admit that everything in life isn't wrong, that you're feeling in perfect condition for the condition you're in and that you don't have a thing of substance to complain about. Good grief. In that case, what's left to talk about, right? A person could get forced to read and think for a change instead. Now there's an illuminating possibility.

March 20: Josh Billings said, "Don't put off till tomorrow what can be enjoyed today." The funny thing about work is that it never goes away. The funny thing about enjoyment is that it does. Get it?

March 21: If you're in the middle of something really unendurable, don't quit. "The unendurable is the beginning of the curve of joy," Djuna Barnes wrote. When you quit enduring the unendurable, in other words, you can finally start living the way you want to live somewhere else or at least someway else that brings you joy.

March 22: Here's a nice one: "A diamond is a chunk of coal that made good under pressure." Think about it. Want a mirror? Check it out.

March 23: They who bind to themselves a joy / Does the winged life destroy; / But they who kiss the joy as it flies / Live in Eternity's sunrise, the poet Blake wrote. And it's true. If you refuse to hold things lightly, you run the risk of clinging to a thing long after it has ceased to be good for you. But what's worse, as long as your hands are full of the past, you can't possibly fully appreciate the present.

March 24: Here's what's wrong with most of the world. They have either never acted foolishly — how sad — or they have forgotten that they did because they certainly take everybody else's foolishness far too seriously. And they're irritating the life out of us foolish ones.

March 25: Aw, lighten up.

March 26: The psalmist is talking about joy, not about pleasure. Joy, you realize, is simply that deep-down, ever-present, unassailable, and totally un-quenchable voice inside ourselves that looks at life as it is for us and says — "So far, so good."

March 27: People who are full of joy are people who are full of possibility, who live with very few absolutes in their heads, who figure that nothing is quite as bad and most things are far better than we ever take the time to admit.

March 28: It is possible to concentrate too much on the cross if we do not concentrate just as much on the resurrection. God did not will Jesus to die. God simply surrendered Jesus to us and our institutions, death-dealing as they are at times. No, what God willed for Jesus was resurrection and that, we too often forget, is precisely what God wills for us. So rise, why don't you?

March 29: "Color," the painter Claude Monet wrote, "is my day-long obsession, joy, and torment." What a wonderful way to live: to love what I am doing so much that it is my obsession, my joy, and my suffering. The next time you find yourself discouraged ask yourself if what discourages you has also given you equivalent joy. It's worth it then, isn't it?

March 30: "Weeping may endure for a night, but joy comes in the morning," scripture reminds us. Everything passes away, in other words. What do you wish you were not going through right now? Relax, it's temporary.

March 31: "This is the true joy in life, the being used for a purpose recognized by yourself as a mighty one; the being thoroughly worn out before you are thrown on the scrap heap; the being a force of nature instead of a feverish selfish little clod of ailments and grievances complaining that the world will not devote itself to making you happy," George Bernard Shaw wrote. Go ahead, improve on that one, I dare you.

APRIL

Psalm 71

It is you alone
who are my hope,
my trust from my youth.
On you I have relied
from birth;
from the womb you
have been my help.
Constant has been
my hope in you.

*H*ope and despair are not opposites. They are cut from the very same cloth, made from the very same material, shaped from the very same circumstances. Most of all, every life finds itself forced to choose one from the other, one day at a time, one circumstance after another. The only difference between the two is that despair shapes an attitude of mind; hope creates a quality of soul. Despair colors the way we look at things, makes us suspicious of the future, makes us negative about the present. Hope, on the other hand, takes life on its own terms, knows that whatever happens God lives in it, and expects that, whatever its twists and turns, it will ultimately yield its good to those who live it well.

When tragedy strikes, when trouble comes, when life disappoints us, we stand at the crossroads between hope and despair, torn and hurting. Despair cements us in the present; hope sends us dancing around dark corners trusting in a tomorrow we cannot see. Despair says that there is no place to go but here. Hope says that God is waiting for us someplace else. Begin again.

April 1: The basic difference between hope and despair is that hope is defeat that holds on in faith when it is clear that holding on is senseless. "When you get to the end of your rope, tie a knot and hang on," the graffiti says. Can you say it better?

April 2: Who has not known the heavy greyness of despair? It marks most stages of major life change; it signals endings; it challenges beginnings that are beyond our strength. But most of all, perhaps, it tests our mettle. People who learn to walk with despair are the really great people of life. They know that what they are doing is hopeless — and they do it anyway. Despair can be great virtue.

April 3: The reason we despair is because we are inclined to want life on our time instead of on God's time. Just because we do not get what we are working for now does not mean that the work is useless. It just means that what we are working for is not coming now. So? Who said it should?

April 4: The beauty of spiritual blackness is that when the light comes back into our lives, we know it. Pity those who have yet to learn the difference. Those types miss jonquils in spring and stars at night and the laughter of the children next door.

April 5: Never try to talk a person out of their despair. That only proves that you don't really understand it. Instead, simply be in it with them like a mountain climber tethered to a friend below, not to carry them but to break the fall.

April 6: Despair is what throws us on God, humble and full of trust. It is an actual grace in the spiritual life.

April 7: Think for a moment of a time in your life when depression, despair, and dull, dull hopelessness had you caught in its sticky web. What is it in your life right now that threatens to grip you like that again? Is it the same kind of fear that took hold of you the last time? In that case, don't worry about the circumstances. They aren't your problem. Concentrate on exorcising the fear itself. After all, it wasn't true the last time, was it?

April 8: Despair is a very subtle emotion. It masquerades as reality, when, as a matter of fact, it is simply reality exaggerated.

April 9: "This apple has a worm in it," is one way of looking at life. "Look! I got two things: a worm and an apple!" is another. Despair is the first option; the kind of amusement that comes with experience is the other. Choose.

April 10: Things don't defeat us. People don't destroy us. Ideas don't stop us. Despair does. And despair is what comes from inside of us, not from outside of us. In the final analysis, the only question is whether or not I am able to conquer the enemy in myself rather than wear myself out flailing at the little tin enemies outside of me.

April 11: When I say that I am in despair, I am really saying that I have given up on God. Isn't that pathetic? I give up on the only hope I can really count on. Despair says that I am god and if I can't do anything about this situation then nothing and nobody can. An idea like that would be funny if it weren't so ridiculously small-minded.

April 12: When I am in a state of despair, the only answer is the answer of the psalmist: we must turn ourselves to God, give ourselves over to trust, and then hang on with all our might to whatever little glimmers of life we can still feel around us.

April 13: The sunflower is the patron saint of those in despair. When darkness descends on the soul, it is time, like the sunflower, to go looking for whatever good things in life bring us comfort. Then we need music and hobbies and friends and fun and new thoughts, not alcohol and wild nights and immersion in the pain that is killing us. The worst thing is to dull the pain instead of displacing it with the kind of joy or comfort that makes us new. "Give light and the darkness will disappear of itself," the philosopher Erasmus wrote.

April 14: Despair is simply another form of fatigue. We try so hard to do something and nothing happens, so we collapse in the sorrow and shame of failure. Mountain streams, on the other hand, always take the line of least resistance around the rocks and boulders. I'm convinced there's something in that process that all of us need to learn. Have any idea what that might be?

April 15: There is nothing on earth that doesn't look dead just before it sprouts. What is coming to life in you that feels like despair right now?

April 16: Easter is the celebration of hope over despair. The tomb from which Jesus rises is the one we call our heart. Is hope, life, Jesus, dead or alive in your heart now? What would it take for you to rise? Do it. The world depends on the Christ rising in you as much as it ever did on the opening of the tomb in Jerusalem.

April 17: The virtue of hope is more than the process of wishing. Hope is the certainty that what God must do, God will do — provided I do my part to enable it, of course.

April 18: "Turn your face to the sun and the shadows fall always behind you," the native peoples of New Zealand say. When despair comes, in order to dispel it with hope, we have to make the effort. We can't just sit and wait for things outside of us to get better. We have to get better inside about what's going on outside.

April 19: This month's psalm verse is one of my favorites. Here's my loose translation of it: "I may not be much; but you promised...and I believe you." It saves me from having to think that the whole responsibility for anything is mine, an idea that would drive any sane person to despair — a wholly appropriate response in that case, incidentally.

April 20: The problem is that we always think of hope as grounded in the future. Wrong. Hope is always grounded in the past. Hope simply challenges us to remember, always, that we have survived everything in life to this point — and in even better shape often than we were when our troubles began. So why not this situation, too? Hope. You have no reason not to.

April 21: "We turn to God when our foundations are shaking," Charles West writes, "only to find out that it is God who is shaking them." Now that simplifies things. All I need to know is what I am supposed to be learning from this. As soon as you catch on, the ground under you will settle again. What's taking you so long?

April 22: God is not a masochist. God did not send Jesus to get him killed. God sent Jesus to be the loving face of eternity and our institutions killed him. God raised him up so that the work of God could go on. Now that's the kind of God you can hope in. This is a God in whom love conquers evil. Eventually. Wait.

April 23: Hope sings. Hope keeps on keeping on. Hope refuses to die. Hope just smiles and smiles and smiles. Sappy? Maybe, but comedy outdraws tragedy any day. Why? Because hope is the elixir of the human spirit, that's why.

April 24: Hope is what sits by a window and waits for one more dawn, despite the fact that there isn't an ounce of proof that we will get it.

April 25: The nice thing about despair is that it is hard to stay in that state permanently. Pretty soon things get so bad that we are driven to hope. "You must go on, I can't go on, I'll go on," Samuel Beckett writes. That's hope: the willingness to do what can't be done.

April 26: In Ireland, they say, it only rains twice a week — three days the first time and four days the second time. Now that is what some people call "a positive attitude." I call it despair deprived of triumph, hope to the highest power.

April 27: It's the Easter season, the time when we recognize officially that despair is part of life and that hope reigns relentless. Think of the disciples: a whimpering crowd of gutless wonders, if ever there was one, become strong in hope because what they thought would destroy them did not. What have you survived in life, because of which you became stronger and every other difficulty in your life became the stuff of hope? Never forget that though hope conquers despair, yes, despair feeds the hope as well.

April 28: The first spring flower you see say to yourself over and over again: hope rages, hope rages, hope rages in this world. Then ask yourself: and what am I doing to make it real?

April 29: Thinking of hope as a virtue in a world that thinks of hope as the fancy of dreamers and children turns religion upside down. Without hope, evil is a state of life and failure is a given. With hope, no amount of failure is an excuse to despair. "Constant has been my hope in you," the psalmist says. "Constant." Whatever you regret in life, whatever you have done that you fear, put it down; hope in God, be at peace. Constantly.

April 30: The poet Emily Dickinson wrote: *Hope is the thing with feathers / That perches in the soul — / And sings the tune without words / And never stops — at all.* When despair comes, when the bedrock certainty that God has given to us everything we need to live a full and happy life begins to pale, when what we do not have is worth more to us than what we do have, then is precisely the time to rise from the graves we have dug for ourselves and sing. Singing when there is nothing of our making to sing about — now that is hope.

MAY

PSALM 150

Let everything
that has breath
burst into shouts of joy.
With resounding cymbals and drums,
let all sing praise
to God.

*D*on't take beauty for granted. It is sometimes found in the ugliest places, sometimes lost in the richest, sometimes forgotten in the dullest, always abandoned when what is most effective is preferred to what is most soulful. The psalmist asks us to look again at life, to be seduced by beauty, to go wild with the love of life and agog at the gift of it. The psalmist asks us to concentrate on beauty. Imagine what would happen to our lives if we ever did it.

May 1: Bealtaine (Be-all-ta-na) is an old May Day Irish festival that welcomes the beginning of the summer season with the decorating of bushes and the lighting of bonfires. Think of it: a festival to mark the coming of another new kind of beauty in life. This month, put a bow on the plant or bush or tree that is closest to the door of your house. Then, every time you pass it in the next few weeks, praise God for the beauty that comes naturally and regularly into your life — despite the fact that, far too often, you forget to notice it. *Happy Bealtaine.*

May 2: We believe in work. We commit ourselves to people. We give ourselves up to schedules. We even play. What we spend far too little time on is beauty.

May 3: "Beauty is in the eye of the beholder," the poet writes. So, here's the question: is beauty a property found in the thing itself, like color or speed or weight, or is it simply in the evaluation of the person who sees it? Is a thing really beautiful, in other words, or is it beautiful only if I think it is? Think about it. It could make all the difference in the world to your life.

May 4: Is there a difference between what is beautiful, what is popular, and what is pleasing? Are the

Beatles and Beethoven equally beautiful? Is either of them beautiful? Who decides? The answer may not be nearly as important as the willingness to spend time on the question itself.

May 5: No matter how perfect the symphony, how excellent the painting, how compelling the writing, how magnificent the scene, if we fail to develop a lifestyle and a heart that nourishes itself on beauty, life will be barren for us indeed. Beauty lies all around us. It simply waits daily to be born in us.

May 6: Listen to a piece of classical music this month or go to an art gallery or read a poem or pick a flower. Then, ask yourself what kind of beauty doing something like that gives you that is missing from other parts of your life. Now, if you're really brave, ask why you do so little of it.

May 7: Today is the birthday of Johannes Brahms, one of the finest musicians of all times. Now this suggestion will take some doing, I realize, but what the heck, we spend all sorts of time on lesser things in life. This month, find a tape or CD of Brahms's music and play it until you can hum it. Now see? You have a beauty in your soul that nothing and no one can take from you.

May 8: God gave us beauty to enable us to bear the pallid, the humdrum, the downright dullness of the ordinary. Here's the catch: you have to look for it.

May 9: The function of spring is to breathe new life into the human soul. It teaches us to be prepared for beauty just when we least expect it.

May 10: The artist is the person who sees beauty where we do not. Put a new piece of art on your desk, your end table, your wall this month. Look at it every day and ask yourself what of life you see in it that you have too often failed to see.

May 11: To pollute the soul with so much noise or busyness or people that we fail to notice the beauty around us deafens the heart and dulls the senses. Take fifteen minutes and sit someplace alone in perfect silence today. Do nothing. Read nothing. Plan nothing. Just sit. Pick out the most beautiful thing in the room, look at it, and let the sheer existence of it drive out all the clutter in your soul. A garden would be a nice place, or the back of a church maybe, or, better yet, your own living room, kitchen, or bedroom. Stop the world for those few minutes. See how beautiful it is simply to learn to be in the presence of beauty.

May 12: Look around the room you're in. Is there anything in it simply because it is beautiful? If not, you have only one of two choices: either get something beautiful for the place or flee it like the plague. Places that are barren, sterile, or unharmonious are like acid on the soul. They look harmless but they agitate us to the core.

May 13: What the poor lack most in life, perhaps, is not things; it is beauty. And that is sad. What is just as sad, perhaps, is to be a person who is able to afford beauty but chooses instead to be surrounded only by things that are either purely functional, poorly kept, or totally uncoordinated. Please, as you go through it, add something more to the world than that.

May 14: "It is the gift of all poets," Margery Sharp wrote, "to find the commonplace astonishing, and the astonishing commonplace." It is also the life task of the rest of us. Otherwise, our minds will go to mush and our souls to the sensitivity of robots. Or are you there already?

May 15: Learning to give praise is simply the art of learning to see and hear and note the beauty around us. As you walk from one place to another today, identify three things that bring beauty to the world. Then smile.

May 16: Artists and writers and musicians force us to pause a little to taste the juices of life while we are busy rushing past the present to get always to the future. Lean on them. Otherwise, life could well pass you by and leave you half dead before you ever begin to live at all.

May 17: Beauty is not a waste of time. It nourishes the soul and stretches us beyond time to those qualities that never fade — order, balance, harmony, insight, uniqueness. How long has it been since you've spent a day in an art gallery, gone to a concert, read a great, great book, gone to a play, walked through a long field to nowhere? Ah, that's too bad. If I were you, I'd confess that. It's a sin of omission that leads to the loss of the best of the self.

May 18: Don't be fooled: beauty is hardly ever explosive, never garish, seldom pretty, little comely. It hides itself behind the ordinary until we ourselves have soul enough to recognize it.

May 19: Now here's a thought: "The power that makes grass grow, fruit ripen, and guides the bird in flight is in us all," Anzia Yezierska says. Now tell me again: what lack in you is it that makes you so afraid of life?

May 20: Beauty is anything that engages our minds or captures our souls in such a way that, after that experience, we are softer, sharper, more understanding, more human, human beings.

May 21: Beauty doesn't just happen to us. We have to dispose our souls to see it. Hitler may have known art, for instance, but he clearly had no capacity for beauty. The artist has the moral obligation to do art. Emile Zola wrote, "If you ask me what I came to do in this world, I, an artist, I will answer you: 'I am here to live out loud.'" But the artists of the world cannot see for us unless we allow ourselves to look through those eyes; the musicians cannot call us to new spiritual heights unless we are willing to hear what they hear; the writers cannot think new thoughts for us unless we are willing to immerse ourselves in those ideas. We have the moral obligation to prepare our hearts to receive the gift of insight that they are sent to give us. That's the function of beauty: to enable us to see and hear and think newly all the time. Do something beautiful today.

May 22: Be careful that you don't confuse "beauty" with "prettiness." A thing is "pretty" if it looks pleasing. A thing is "beautiful" if it stops us in mid-air and makes us add something to a subject we thought we already knew everything there was to know about it.

May 23: Beauty steeps us in the highest levels of human thought and possibility. It is not a luxury. It is a necessity. Without it, a person can never be fully human. To rape the land, to concentrate only on production, profit, and the basest elements of survival dehumanize life. If you don't believe that, just look at how poverty, garbage, noise pollution, pornography, and junk are choking the life out of us now. Don't think for a minute that we can live without beauty. It's time for beauty to be discovered again.

May 24: The psalmist knows what most of us spend our lifetime to discover: what God wills for humankind is beauty. Too often we miss it, ignore it, or take it for granted. Too seldom do we become the paeans of praise that the psalmist requires. Who's more real, do you think — people like us for whom beauty has become a rarity of life or the psalmist who lives in a symphony of praise?

May 25: The poet William Allingham writes about the beauties of his life: *Two ducks on the pond / a grass bank beyond / a blue sky of spring / White birds on the wing: What a little thing / To remember for years / To remember with tears!* What are the beauties of yours? Write them down today and put the list in your wallet. After all, those are very valuable things.

May 26: Imagine a day without something to drink, a week without food, a month without weekends. You'd never do that to your body. But we go for days without good music, for weeks without good reading, for months without sitting under a tree, and for years without visiting a single art gallery. In just those ways the soul shrinks to the ineffective, the inhuman, the intolerably boring.

May 27: It's the beauty within us that makes it possible for us to recognize the beauty around us. You know what that means, don't you? If we want beauty to pervade the world, we are going to have to provide it; we'll have to express it first in ourselves. "The work of art which I do not make, none other will ever make it," Simone Weil warns us. Provide someone around you with a bit of beauty today.

May 28: "Art," Elizabeth Brown wrote, "is the only thing that can go on mattering once it has stopped hurting." Real beauty breaks us open to what we've never known before. Beauty changes us.

May 29: "One of the most difficult things to do," the artist Vincent Van Gogh said, "is to paint darkness which nonetheless has light in it." That's what beauty does to life: it brings a shaft of light into darkness, the order of melody to chaos, the insights of poetry to prose, a glimpse of the essential under the cosmetics of life. As Van Gogh teaches us, beauty is something we have to work at or the darkness of life will take over.

May 30: Today is the feast of Joan of Arc. Her refusal to betray her inner voices simply to curry favor with the authorities who were threatened by her visions was the kind of beauty, the kind of creativity that changes life for the rest of the world.

May 31: "All are but parts of one stupendous whole, Whose body Nature is, and God the soul," Alexander Pope wrote. But it wasn't an earth-shattering discovery. The psalmist clearly knew it before Pope did. The question is, do you? If so, then you already know the secret of beauty; you are ready to respect the beauty around you; most of all, you can, with confidence, release your own. Then, life itself becomes beautiful whatever the dull times, the ugly times that threaten it. It's the beauty we develop in ourselves — the depth of soul, the symphonic ear, the visionary eye, the natural softness we've learned from the lessons of life — that enables us to see it in other places.

JUNE

PSALM 102

You, O God, are kind
and full of compassion,
slow to anger,
abounding in love.
You are good to all,
compassionate
to all your creatures.

There's no use trying. It can't be done. No one can go through life alone. We're made incomplete. We always want something outside ourselves that only someone else can supply. The problem is that there's a very delicate balance between needing another and being enough for ourselves. There is a very delicate balance between depending on the people in our lives and learning to depend on God. Life is the process of coming to realize the implications of those things. When we depend too much on another person we lose something in ourselves. When we make ourselves the beginning and the end of our own small world, we starve ourselves of the beauty in others. When we fail to develop a relationship with God we wither on the human vine. The results of all those skewed relationships are psychologically devastating. Clearly the psalmist, in talking about love and compassion and the presence of God, touches a very raw nerve — and gives us a clue to its resolution.

June 1: Loneliness and dependency are opposite poles of the same axle. It's one thing to miss a person when that person is not with us; it's another thing to be incapable of functioning without that person. Unless I keep myself for myself, I have absolutely nothing to give to another that can possibly enrich the other's own life. Being an albatross around someone's neck is not a relationship; it's a trap.

June 2: Don't be afraid to be lonely. Loneliness teaches us what we lack — and what we don't. Loneliness is a short course in personal development.

June 3: It isn't just companionship we need. It's a sense of security, of being cared about, of being known. Human relationships are God's way of being there for us when night comes to the soul.

June 4: To have something to give another, we have to have something of substance in ourselves. We have to have a spiritual life that makes sense out of dailiness. We need to know God if we ever, ever hope to be able to love another person well. Otherwise we cling; otherwise we live down to lesser things.

June 5: The greatest question of life is what to do when a relationship fails. The answer is to have developed a life beforehand rich enough to make life possible even in the midst of loss.

June 6: Don't ask yourself how another person failed you. Ask yourself why it is that you look to other people to satisfy all your needs for fun and fulfillment in the first place.

June 7: When your partner is late for supper, eat. When your partner doesn't want to go to the theater, ask someone else to go. When your partner doesn't enjoy what you enjoy, join a group that does. Or, translated: don't blame someone else for making you unhappy. Get a life.

June 8: If you could spend three nights alone this week, what three different things would you do? How long has it been since you've done them? Why not? Don't miss the point: there's a clue in that about what's wrong with your life right now. Change it — if you don't want to be dead before they bury you, that is.

June 9: Compassion consists of doing something loving for someone you would not ordinarily love. Like God was with the Israelites. Like God is with you. Agreed? Good. Now name ten people to whom you have been compassionate. Five? Three? Anybody? Go find somebody. Now.

June 10: It's possible to be lonely all our lives and never even really know that something we badly need is missing. We go into a kind of low-level spiritual coma and simply keep on keeping on, too numbed out to know we're not really happy. Then we need to take inventory. Don't ask, "Who's missing?" Ask "What's missing?" Then take responsibility for your soul and go get it.

June 11: No one who really loves you expects you to be there all the time. That's called smothering. "I always felt that the great high privilege, relief and comfort of friendship," Katherine Mansfield wrote, "was that one had to explain nothing." Until you're free to come and go from the presence of a friend, without explanation, without permission, without devastation, you're not free at all.

June 12:   Loneliness scours the soul of self-centeredness. It's good to be able to miss another person. It tempers arrogance, it diminishes our tendency to assume, it makes us human. That's why we let people into our lives in the first place; they bring the power to leave us lonely.

June 13:   Beware of your own emotional maturity if you've never been lonely. You may never have loved anyone but yourself. What a pitiable love life that would be.

June 14:   Loneliness is the only measure we have of our capacity for God. The greater the size of the hole in our heart when we lose someone we love, so great indeed is our talent for the love that never goes away.

June 15:   Without a spiritual life, the loss of life's beacons can devastate us. When our heart is plumbed to the presence of God, on the other hand, there is nothing we can lose that can really devastate us, because then God will have become all we need.

June 16:   "Take your life in your own hands, and what happens?" Erica Jong writes. "A terrible thing: no one to blame." Think about it. Chilling, isn't it?

June 17: Don't expect to find God once you lose the human things of life. What you do not have now, you will not have then.

June 18: God's compassion is not to be confused with Disney World. God does not give us a marshmallow life. God gives us life in all its learnings. God's compassion simply means that God will be there with us in all of them.

June 19: God loves us in a way no human can. God loves us enough to know that we are capable of losing everything and becoming happier all the time, of being on our own and being safe.

June 20: Beware of those relationships that capture all your time, take all your energy, expect all your attention, and fear your independence. They are not of God because they don't leave any space for all the other things in life God gives us for our growth.

June 21: "Loneliness is the poverty of self; solitude is the richness of self," the poet May Sarton wrote. When I feel lonely it is because something is missing in me. When I am alone and satisfied it is because there is something very much alive in me. The trick is to feed the spirit until being alone is a happy privilege and not a deprivation.

June 22: When I concentrate too much on someone else, I fail to develop something eternal in myself. Then, when I find myself alone, I have no resources to draw from. What a pity. It isn't that life has passed me by; it's that I passed life by along the way — and never even noticed.

June 23: Love is something that comes like lightning and stays only if it's nourished. The spiritual truth is that God comes to us like a flash of light and waits for us to notice. Devastating loneliness, ruinous dependency are sure signs that we haven't.

June 24: Else Lasker-Schuler wrote: "My love for you is the sole image of God a human is allowed." Look into the face of the person you love today. What do you see there of God? What gift have you been given in this person?

June 25: No single person can satisfy all our needs, all our desires. If there is anything wrong with the idea of marriage today, the idea that we can be everything that the beloved needs is surely it. Make yourself a world so that you are interesting enough to be around, adult enough to be alone, not a burden.

June 26: God loves you enough to allow you to be independent. Have you done the same for anyone else?

June 27: We want compassion for ourselves and justice for the poor, a *Covenant of Care* for ourselves and *Contract with America* for everybody else. How far away from the com-passion of God we really are. And we call ourselves Christian and this a "Christian" nation. It would be funny if it weren't so tragic.

June 28: "Love doesn't just sit there, like a stone. It has to be made, like bread, re-made all the time, made new," Ursula LeGuin wrote. That's why we're told to pray every day. That's why we keep saying "I love you." That's why we need to make sure that we do something loving for the people we say we love every single day of our lives. And when was the last time you did that for anyone? (P.S.: Birthdays and Christmas don't count.)

June 29: Agnes Repplier wrote, "It is not easy to find happiness in ourselves, and impossible to find it elsewhere." Here's the question: what is too much dependence? Here's the better question: what is too much independence? Go ahead, you know the answer. You can figure it out.

June 30: "To love deeply in one direction makes us more loving in all others," Anne-Sophie Swetchine says. Don't be afraid when someone you love loves someone else, too. So does God — and that works.

JULY

Psalm 139

Before even a word
is on my tongue,
you know it
through and through.
Your presence
surrounds me;
your blessing
is ever upon me.
Too wonderful for me,
this knowledge,
too high, beyond my reach.

We *spend our whole lives, some of us, try-ing to understand who and what we are. Some of the rest of us spend little or no time on that topic at all.*

One extreme is narcissism. The other extreme is self-effacement to the point of invisibility — even to ourselves.

Neither extreme is healthy, of course, but a bit of each is a good idea. The psalmist figured out long before we that life is both a giddy excursion into the sustaining mind of God and a thought far too exalted to begin to be grasped. So, sometimes we feel completely invincible and sometimes we feel completely powerless. It all depends on whether we have a sense of being immersed in God or not. Sometimes I think it depends on whether it's Monday or Friday.

At any rate, God is present in our lives, but it takes a lot of reflection sometimes to realize that. On the other hand, sometimes we aren't wonderful at all, and it takes a lot of denial to bear that. Full human development may, in the end, depend on only two things: first, that we al-ways remember ourselves at our worst and, second, that we never forget ourselves at our best. Knowing who we are, really, ranks with life's greatest gifts and most hum-bling experiences at the same time. To achieve that kind of self-knowledge, that escape from denial, God gives us memories, reflection, and a sense of divine presence in life.

July 1: "One may understand the cosmos, but never the ego; the self is more distant than any star," G. K. Chesterton said. Name three things you did within the last week. Tell yourself why you did each of them. Now tell yourself the real reason you did them. That's what's really driving you. Do you like it?

July 2: Name three things that you really wish you had not done in life. What did you learn in each instance that made you a better person thereafter? Then what are you ashamed about? You grew up a little more every time, didn't you? After all, going back to God a shallow-souled child is not much of a human accomplishment.

July 3: In every one of us there is what psychologists call "the inner dialogue" going on all the time. We talk to ourselves about ourselves. Constantly. Monitor those conversations very closely today. What are you saying to yourself? What does it have to do with the way you feel about yourself? Here's a good idea: change the channel every once in a while. Think of something outside yourself that is beautiful, good, funny, loving, enjoyable. See what I mean? It's a lot more relaxing.

July 4: Memory is God's apology for distance. Enjoy it.

July 5: Don't confuse self-reflection and self-absorption. Self-absorption is that state of soul in which we see, evaluate, and respond to all other situations solely out of self-interest. Self-reflection is when we ask ourselves why we are doing what we are doing? J. P. Morgan said once that there are always two reasons for doing everything: the good reason and the real reason. Self-reflection happens when you check your reasons. Do you like why you are doing what you are doing now? Be careful. This reason will be the basis for your future mental health.

July 6: With the advent of the ecological moment, Thomas Berry teaches, we are moving from a concentration on redemption to an emphasis on creation. That means that we'll begin to be less concerned with sin and more concerned with life-fulfillment. Are you doing what you know down deep that you should be doing with your life? What's stopping you? It may be worth the loss — but only if you agree that this is the way you prefer to live. Do you?

July 7: To say that public hate-mongering in the name of radio talk shows doesn't create the climate for racism, sexism, the bombing of federal buildings, and international political thuggery, as well, is to deny the fact that behavior has consequences. Self-reflection demands that we ask ourselves what we ourselves are contributing to the social environment: human hatreds or human community. Careful: think of your last three conversations with neighbors, friends, family. What did you talk about? What did you yourself add to the conversation?

July 8: It's so easy to refuse to take personal responsibility for the good order of the world around us. But if we do that we cease to be blessing and begin to be a burden on the universe. And that, surely, is the real meaning of sin.

July 9: The presence of God comes subtly: in the voices of those we love, in the burst of new flowers, in awesome acts of generosity. Where was God for you yesterday? You could be that for someone today. Why not?

July 10: Count your blessings today. I'm serious. Count them — and don't leave any of them out. Now, tell me again: why are you complaining?

July 11: We cannot know the presence of God without coming to know ourselves as well. Why? Because we really feel God only in those areas in which we are at both our strongest and our weakest selves.

July 12: There is such a temptation in our age to see the universe as a huge machine that is self-impelling and without spiritual presence. Well, then, if it is, why can't we control it? The truth is that we have made ourselves God — and it didn't work. Maybe that's why the spiritual life is so difficult for us. We want to run everything without reference to anything greater than ourselves. We never give in to life.

July 13: It isn't that God disappears from us. It is that we have disappeared from God. We've given up the daily, daily search for God in life. Be honest with yourself: have you consciously attended to your spiritual life any time this week? Hmmmmmm? And then we wonder why life seems so dangerous, so empty, so destructive.

July 14: As far as the psalmist was concerned, God was the giver of blessings. Who is God for you? A dour old man who waits in heaven to see if we'll finally get there? Or the one who smiles at us all the way through life, the God the psalmist talks about? If I were you, I'd trust the psalmist's image of God more than I do the ideas of those who live in fear and punishment. They make God more in their own image and likeness than in the obvious vision of the one who goes on pouring out life and goodness and beauty, even when we miss it, day after day after day.

July 15: "One good memory may be the means of saving us," Dostoyevsky wrote. And he's right. For instance, name three of the best things you've ever done in your life. Now see what memory does? It feeds the notion that tomorrow can be good because yesterday was. Isn't that a nice grace on a bad day?

July 16: "Learn what you are and be such," Pindar said. Now hear this: learning what we are is the hard part. We spend our young lives trying to be someone else, our middle age pretending to be what other people think we are, and old age trying to give ourselves permission to be and do what we have wanted to do for years. How do you do it? Easy, just do this:

every time someone wants you to do something, just ask yourself, "Do I really want to do this?" And if you don't, don't.

July 17: Don't be afraid to be who you are, no matter who wants you to be otherwise for whatever reason. Life is for those who live it. Anything else is a poor copy of a bad idea.

July 18: The question is not, "Is God present to us?" The question is, "Are we present to God?"

July 19: Remember the crisis from which you thought you'd never recover. What happened? That's what I thought. That's why older people are so serene. They know that absolutely everything turns out right. Eventually.

July 20: When God promised to be with us till the end of time, God did not promise to be Santa Claus. God promised to be God. Have you lived long enough to know the difference yet? What is it?

July 21: The psalmist makes it very clear: we are known to God through and through. So what is life all about? Easy: God is giving us the time to come to know ourselves, to rejoice in our own creation, to grow to its limits. Isn't that wonderful? God's best gift to ourselves is — ourselves.

July 22: The next time someone does something to you that you don't like, don't spend your energy being angry at the other person. Instead, ask yourself the question, "What am I doing to evoke that kind of response?" You'll learn plenty about yourself. That's called self-reflection. Try it; it works.

July 23: Here's what's good for memory: amnesia. Quit thinking about all the bad things in your life. You're wasting time.

July 24: H. L. Mencken defined Puritanism as "the lurking fear that someone, somewhere, may be having a good time." The psalmist, on the other hand, clearly assumes that the eleventh commandment is to enjoy the party, any party, every party. Stick with psalmists.

July 25: The first half of life we spend trying to make it a good one. The second half of life we realize that it is.

July 26: How do you know when you have finally achieved a sense of the presence of God? Simple: you cease to live for what you don't already have; you cease to be afraid of what you can't control in life; you cease to feel guilty for being yourself. It's a great moment. Cultivate it.

July 27: God, the psalmist says, knows everything there is to know about us — and loves us anyway. So now what are you worried about?

July 28: The purpose of self-reflection is not perfection. There is no such thing. The notion of perfection is simply a by-product of human arrogance. The purpose of self-reflection is self-acceptance. Until we know what we are and can accept the struggle of it, we can never love anyone else fully.

July 29: God knows our inner struggles and loves us for them. Struggle, after all, is the sign that we care.

July 30: It's so comforting to know that God already knows everything about us. Nothing we do can be a surprise then. Except, of course, to ourselves. And that is the most shocking revelation of them all — and the most developmental.

July 31: Woody Allen said once, "I don't believe in an after-life — but I'm taking a change of underwear just in case." Self-reflection is when we know that we don't yet know it all and are open to learning something new about life. What are you most sure of right now that you're not sure you're sure of, come to think about it? That's okay. A little ambiguity is good for the soul. After all, God is, and that's enough.

AUGUST

PSALM 59

O my Strength,
it is you
to whom I turn,
for you are my refuge,
the God who
shows me love.

*L*ieutenant Scott O'Grady, the young American flyer shot down over Bosnia, was, by his own description, "a scared rabbit" who sobbed when, after six days of hiding in the mountains, he was finally rescued by U.S. Marines. The country, however, called him "heroic." The situation is a wild departure in the use of the term "heroic" as we usually imagine it. It does not fit, for instance, the conventional Superman prototype of courage, the macho model of strength, the take-control convention of manliness, the stereotypical stoicism of the St. Cecilias of the world who brave dismemberment without a whimper. Never doubt it for a moment, though: the customary images are wrong; the instincts of the country are right. Courage is not the ability to face danger without hesitation; strength is not the suppression of human emotion. Courage is simply the ability to survive weakness; strength is only the ability to weather fear.

In fact, if truth were known, courage and strength may simply be the by-products of peril, not the internal arsenal we build up to defend ourselves against it at all. Courage and strength may come after the fact. Once we've been scared to death by something and bested it may be when we really get courage. Once we've found out that strength is something that comes from faith, once we've braved the worst that life can deal us and endured it — then may be when we discover that we have become strong, not because of ourselves, but despite ourselves.

The psalmist says it very well: we are not strong at all. God is. It's a very liberating thought. It means that we can all get up tomorrow. There is nothing at all that can take us down as long as God is in our lives.

August 1: Fear, like pain, is a beautiful thing. Pain tells us what it is in us that hurts so that we can heal it before it destroys us. Fear signals to us where we need help before we attempt to take on a world that is so much bigger than we are.

August 2: To be afraid of something is to have the wisdom to examine it closely, to study it well, to prepare for it carefully so that when we do move we are equal to the task.

August 3: Fear is what throws us back on God. Say the psalm verse again and give praise for the fears in you. Without them you might never come to know God at all.

August 4: Courage is what keeps us trying to do things at which we are very likely to fail — like walking into a room full of strangers, all of whom are themselves already friends; like speaking up when our principles are compromised; like learning to question both church and state so that our faith is mature and our citizenship is real.

August 5: Courage rests in the willingness to trust ourselves to survive failure. Be careful. It may be precisely the need to succeed that smothers your courage.

August 6: Don't think for a moment that a courageous person is not afraid. On the contrary, people of courage are simply people who do not allow their fears to control their lives. They get on airplanes though they suffer from fear of flying; they speak up in front of people despite the fact that they are shy; they try new things even when they fear to be ridiculed for it; they say hello first, even when they fear they'll be ignored. They are brave enough to stretch themselves one step beyond their comfort level. Do something courageous for yourself today. You'll feel so good about yourself tonight if you do.

August 7: The brave are those who barter their reputations, their friends, and their security for principles and people who cannot defend themselves. Name one situation in your own life in which you were brave. What happened to you as a result?

August 8: Tweedledum says in Lewis Carroll's *Through the Looking-Glass,* "I'm very brave generally, only today I happen to have a headache." And what's your excuse?

August 9:   Cowards are those who take on the thoughts and ideas and directions of whomever they happen to be with at the moment. What a gruesome, tortured way to live. It means you have to stand around waiting to see what you're supposed to think. I had a bishop-friend once who was fond of saying when the conversation got tranquil: "I'm going home now. No one is learning anything anymore. Everybody is agreeing." Dull, isn't it?

August 10:   "Courage without conscience," wrote Robert G. Ingersoll, "is a wild beast." Choose carefully what you're ready to die for, in other words. Don't lay your life down for anything worth less than a life. And while we're at it, why not take a pen and write down what those things would be. Don't worry. It won't be a long, long list.

August 11: It takes great courage to endure the unendurable. Name three people you know who have it. Should the unendurable ever be endured?

August 12: C. S. Lewis wrote: "Courage is not simply one of the virtues but the form of every virtue at the testing point, which means at the point of highest reality." It takes courage to love the unlovable, courage to struggle for justice against unjust odds, courage to keep the faith when the institution shrinks it to a size beneath the gospel vision, courage to have less than we can so that the destitute can have more. And where is such courage today?

August 13: "Some have been thought brave because they were afraid to run away," the English proverb teaches. Now that one I understand. Go ahead: name some grand thing you've been given credit for doing simply because you couldn't get out of it. Isn't that fun? Now you know where God was in your life when you didn't even notice.

August 14: Fear is what takes over when we rely on our own resources. I mean, face it: nobody knows better than we do how really inadequate we are. "Courage is fear that has said its prayers," the wag wrote. Only this time, the wag was a psalmist.

August 15: "Because you have been bitten by a snake, you fear every rope," the Sufi says. What ropes in your life are you treating like snakes? What specific fears have you allowed to transfer to your life?

August 16: Courage happens when the commitment to principle triumphs over the concern for personal advantage.

August 17: Fear is our doorway to the heart of God.

August 18: There is a such a thing as foolish courage. There is also such a thing as holy fear. Some things deserve our concern; some do not. Have you learned the difference between the two yet? Trust me: if you grow to full stature as a person, you will.

August 19: It isn't that some people are so much more courageous than the rest of us. It may be simply that they're smarter. They know that anything that diminishes us as persons is not worth our deference.

August 20: Isn't it funny? When a woman reaches her limit of oppression and gets angry, they call it "hysteria" and give her a pill to get over it. When a man reaches his limits and faces up to his oppressor, they call it "courageous" and give him medals.

August 21: Luis Buñuel wrote: "If we could only find the courage to leave our destiny to chance, to accept the fundamental mystery of our lives, then we might be closer to the sort of happiness that comes with innocence." Which translated means: go with the flow. Try it, why don't you? For one day, just have the courage to take things as they come. Don't despair, don't rant and rave, don't wring your hands. Just learn to love them.

August 22: "Doc," the nervous little man said to the psychiatrist, "every time I get into bed, I begin to see dragons. I've been to doctor after doctor but none of them have helped me a bit. Can you?" "Of course I can," the psychiatrist said, "but the treatment will be very expensive." "Never mind that," the man said, "it's worth it. How much do you want?" "By the time we're through, the entire therapy will cost you at least $150,000," the doctor said. "A hundred fifty thousand?!" the man screamed — incredulously. "Forget it. I'll go home and learn to love the bloody thing." Point: don't get romantic ideas. Sometimes courage is simply learning to endure what we can't change.

August 23: There is nothing on earth that can guard us from loss except an awareness of the presence of God in our lives who is, of course, still everything we need when we have nothing left.

August 24: "Those have not learned the lesson of life who do not every day surmount a fear," Ralph Waldo Emerson wrote. Courage, in other words, is not the gene of giantism; it is the DNA of ordinary moral growth — which means to us common types: if you want to make it, you better do it.

August 25: What's coming up that you're afraid of in life? Reach out right now; take the hand of God; keep going.

August 26: If you're feeling like you're in the midst of something that you'd like to run away from, you're not a coward; you're normal. Cowardice is when you won't even try.

August 27: If God didn't think we could make it all the way to the end, we would all have died a lot younger than we are now. So cheer up. All it takes to be strong is to go on breathing when quitting seems preferable.

August 28: I don't know about you, but I always think of psalmists as being brave. Not this one. This one is my kind of folk. His advice: let God do in you what you cannot do in your life — what you would never be brave enough to do yourself. I agree.

August 29: Are you disturbed about racism, sexism, consumerism, militarism, anything? Good. For your daily moral exercise, say it to someone.

August 30: Courage is the willingness to go on going on when there is not a shred of reason to believe that whatever we are doing will succeed.

August 31: Courage is what's left over when what we wish we did not have to face cannot be avoided. Then the strength we need to be more than we are comes from God. Then life itself becomes the psalm which, until that time, I can only pray exists.

SEPTEMBER

Psalm 69

In your loving kindness,
answer me;
in your compassion,
turn toward me.
Do not hide your face;
answer quickly,
for I am in distress.
Come close and
save me from my foes.

*I*t's not considered "nice," it's not often considered Christian, sometimes it's not even considered healthy to talk about enemies and anger. But the psalmist does. The psalmist is a realist. The psalmist knows what we hate to admit: there are people in our lives we consider enemies. We have moments of irascible anger — the messy kind, the embarrassing kind. And we don't know what to do about it. But the psalmist does. The psalmist seeks God and the psalmist seeks refuge and the psalmist seeks comfort. To deal with anger and enemies properly, we all need the same. Lack any one of those things and anger can poison life like one drop of ink in five gallons of water. Think about it.

September 1: "Anger is an acid that can do more harm to the vessel in which it stands than to anything on which it's poured," the proverb teaches. It boils over inside of us and scorches our souls. It ruins family picnics and office projects and even long-term relationships. We can do one of three things when we're angry: we can explode; we can swallow it and live with it forever; or we can say why we're so upset and explore what's going on in ourselves instead of continuing to concentrate on the other person. You figure out which one is best in the long run.

September 2: The interesting thing about anger is that if we explode at the child who drops the cup, or the worker who's late with the material, nothing happens but more anger. We've known for a long time that "getting it out" only increases it — like the parent who, having raised her voice, can only continue to emphasize the gravity of the situation by raising it even louder the next time. No, exploding doesn't really help at all. Now we just have four problems instead of one: a missed deadline, a broken relationship, a headache, and an irritated soul.

September 3: Anger is often an impetus to change things, but it is never a solution. Think of how much easier it would have been to simply say, "From now on, I want you to use the paper cups," or "It is your responsibility to pay the air express to get this project delivered on time." Think of how much holier your life would be. Oh, yes, I almost forgot. Do it on the spot if you can. Don't stew.

September 4: Political scientists teach that there are no such things as permanent international allies; there are only permanent national needs. First, Germany and Japan were our enemies and China was our friend. Now, Germany and Japan are our greatest trading partners. Then, China was our enemy until Richard Nixon went to visit; and in one weekend years of enmity ended. Russia was certainly our enemy, and now not a word is said about communism though the largest nation on earth, China, is still communist. See what I mean? Be very careful that you don't make judgments about people and nations based on political interests. You will wake up someday with egg all over your face, mud on your soul, and cement in your heart. And that is a very sad way to live.

September 5: Do not make your enemies the center of your life. Life is worth so much more than that. Don't fume it away.

September 6: Try this: think of everyone you dislike, distrust, detest today. As you bring each name to mind say, "Betty, I wish you every good thing your heart desires." Say it over and over again. It is an act of God. See what happens.

September 7: The Russians say, "A thousand friends are few, one enemy is too many." Don't give your life over to your enemies. Let your friends show you the love of God for you in life.

September 8: When you're hurt and angry, tell somebody. That's called spiritual direction. Just don't tell everybody. That's called vindictiveness. The purpose of talking about the hurt is not to maintain it and preserve it and milk it dry. The purpose of talking about past hurt is simply to understand it so that we can deal with it better in the future. It's aimed at changing myself, not the other.

September 9: The value of anger is that it helps us to understand ourselves better. It's not possible to do anything about the others. I can, on the other hand, do something about myself. Anger is often the beginning of a whole new life.

September 10: Beware of cheap forgiveness, the marshmallow stuff that we profess before we have really drained the situation of its deep meaning to us. Cheap forgiveness too often comes back wearing a mask. Then even we ourselves don't know what's the matter with us. The Hindustani say, "Concealed enmity or wickedness comes to light at last." What we do not absolve in ourselves never goes away.

September 11: "It is often the most wicked who know the nearest path to the shrine," the Japanese proverb reminds us. Don't let anybody fool you: goodness is as goodness does. Be careful who you call bad simply because the "good" people have named them so. God, it seems, is far less quick to judge.

September 12: Whatever you do, try not to confuse an enemy with an opponent. An enemy is someone who seeks your harm. An opponent is simply someone with another way of looking at things. Enemies are dangerous. Opponents are necessary to keep us thinking.

September 13: "If we had been holier people, we would have been angrier oftener," Templeton wrote. Believe it: there are things worth being angry at in life — the deprivation of children, the oppression of women, the exploitation of workers, the rape of the earth — just as God was angry at Sinai, as Jesus was angry in the Temple. The trick is to be able to sustain a holy anger that energizes us for change without allowing it to turn us into what we hate.

September 14: The image of the passionless Christian — the sweet, saccharine, flaccid, and passive participant in life — is not worthy of the ideals of Christianity. To know, for instance, that according to the U.S. Budget Office, welfare in all its forms is only 3 percent of the budget and not be angry about the ruthless political attack on the disadvantaged families that receive it in the wealthiest country in the world is to be less than Christian.

September 15: One of the ways that the psalmist deals with anger is to face it in himself. It's amazing how we fear the anger in ourselves so much that we turn it against ourselves in depression, disease, and compulsions and then we turn it against others by our chronic irritations. The point is to face it, resolve it, and get on with life.

September 16: "Anger," William Sloane Coffin wrote, "is what keeps us from tolerating the intolerable." So why, do you suppose, is there so much poverty, so much hunger, so much abuse in the world?

September 17: I am proud of my enemies. They tell me what I stand for. I have earned every one of them; I worked hard to get them; I wouldn't give them up for the world!

September 18: It isn't that we have enemies that is the problem. The problem lies in the fact that either we have not been willing to learn something about ourselves from them or we have not done anything worthwhile enough to merit the right ones. One of the great spiritual questions of life is, "Who would you be willing to have as enemies and have you done anything to deserve them?"

September 19: The psalmist teaches one of the greatest lessons of life: it is not our place to punish our enemies. God will do that. Our place is simply to leave them to God's justice and commend ourselves to God's mercy.

September 20: Faced with his enemies, the psalmist seeks God, seeks help, and seeks comfort — not vengeance, not even justification. It's a good lesson for the rest of us. When we feel under siege, the answer is to trust in God, to let someone help us through its effect on our own life and to concentrate on other things in life — on the things that bring us beauty and joy — not simply on the hurt, the pain, the anger, the resentment that comes from feeling isolated and under attack.

September 21: Buddy Hackett's got the right idea. He says, "Don't carry a grudge. While you're carrying a grudge, the other guy is out dancing." If something hurt you yesterday, in other words, make your happiness somewhere else today. Don't get stuck in the pain of the past.

September 22: The institutionalization of enmity is called war. It's called Rwanda. It's called Bosnia. It's called the Gaza Strip. And we bless it in the name of "justice," but justice is never done by war. The lives of the innocent are always destroyed; the lives of the weapons-makers are always enhanced. How long, O God, how long? As long as people like ourselves keep calling it justice, patriotism, and necessity — that's how long.

September 23: "Anger is a stone cast into a wasp's nest," says a proverb from Malabar. Think about it.

September 24: Being angry is not the issue. Being hurtful is.

September 25: Face it: there are some people you just don't like. Their chemistry and yours are a volatile mix. Christianity does not require that you elope with them: only that you live with them gently, do them no harm, wish them well — and go your own way.

September 26: Don't wish vengeance on your enemies. Wish love on them. It's awfully hard for people to be nasty when they're in love. (I'm convinced that's why primitive cultures did not allow a man to have relations with his wife before battle and why some still closet their athletes before big games.) Love mellows us.

September 27: When you are thinking about your enemies, remember to beware most of all of the one within — the one who concentrates on enemies even when our enemies are far at bay.

September 28: The old axiom, "Pray for your enemies," is not errant pietism. It is both good Christianity and good psychology. It's good Christianity because it turns the other cheek. It's good psychology because it melts our own hearts toward them. And who knows? Maybe they are not the barrier to our relationship. Maybe I am.

September 29: Enemies are a gift from God. They keep us aware of our weaknesses and, when we're finally exhausted by the struggle, they lead us to God.

September 30: "The worst enemies are those whose faces are cheerful," Caecilius writes, "while their hearts are bitter." Be angry if you must, opposed if you will, but never, ever be dishonest about it; never, ever be hypocritical about it or your own soul will wither from a lack of real life.

OCTOBER

PSALM 92

The just will flourish like the palm tree
and grow tall
as Lebanon cedars.
Planted
in your garden,
they will flourish
in your presence.
Still bearing fruit
in old age,
still full of sap,
still green,
They proclaim your constancy.

We live in a strange period in history. As a culture, we get older every day; as a people we become more and more intent on staying young. Not simply on staying alive, mind you, but on staying young. As if being young were somehow or other better than being old. As if any part of life is preferable to any other part. As if age were not an invitation to wisdom. As if age did not have its own beauty, its own joy. The psalmist, however, brings another perspective on age for our consideration. The psalmist says that as we get to be better people, life gets better, too. Not more nimble, perhaps, but better. But if that's true, then that gets to be a major life decision. What do we want to be — nimble or better — as life goes on? Think carefully. The answer is not nearly as easy as it may seem.

October 1: Youth is a period of experimentation. We test all the rules of family, society, and church to see if they're worthwhile. If parents say, "Don't ride your bike on gravel," we do. If society says, "Don't drink and drive," we do. Age is that period of life in which the rules cease to be a collection of regulations and begin to be a choice of values: safety over silliness, responsibility over recklessness. Maybe the purpose of age lies in coming to confirm what humanity has always known so that humanity does not die a premature death.

October 2: They say that the older we get the more cautious we get. I don't think so. I think the older we get the smarter we get. We know now what isn't worth the price of a life well-lived.

October 3: I talked to a limo driver in his mid-fifties last week who told me that he had regular customers who envy his job. "I work about five hours a day," he said. "That gives me enough money to live on. Then I go home and barbecue in the back yard. Anything else is greed." I'm still thinking about that. Was that wisdom or was that nonsense? And how do we know the difference?

October 4: Wisdom is what lasts after the experience ends. What was your last major experience? In what way are you wiser because of it? Think carefully. I don't mean more cynical. I mean wiser.

October 5: "A person is not old," Jean Rostand wrote, "as long as they are still seeking something." It's only when we sit back and let life go by that age sets in. What's your next dream in life? If you can't answer that question, get one.

October 6: One of the spiritual diseases of this culture is its youth-centeredness. We don't give age credit for wisdom and we don't give youth credit for needing any; so we pressure the young and degrade the old. That's a crippled society by any measure.

October 7: Ageism is the notion that human intelligence declines in inverse proportion to the increase in arthritis. Ageism just proves how little we really know about life when we're young.

October 8: We've gone in this society from disposing of slightly used Styrofoam cups to disposing of slightly used people. It may be time to recycle our thinking as well as our cups.

October 9: We used to teach people to think about the great questions of life — about the meaning of life and the flow of history and the nature of humanity. Now we teach them to do things. No wonder they don't know how to think about what they do. No wonder we're a society of slippery business deals and technological violence.

October 10: One of the nice things about being young is the fact that making mistakes is taken for granted. Life is one long learning process. The only thing that ruins it is to think otherwise. Then, we condemn ourselves either to perpetual failure or to terminal arrogance. We have to learn to learn.

October 11: How do we explain the amazing affinity between the very old and the very young? Maybe it's because they're both smart enough to pay more attention to what they're doing now than to where they're trying to get in the future. Maybe we should all try it for awhile.

October 12: James A. Garfield wrote, "If wrinkles must be written upon your brows, let them not be written upon the heart. The spirit should never grow old." There's nothing wrong with getting older.

There's plenty wrong with getting sour. When did you do something different last? Go ahead, risk it. Freshen your life. Start over.

October 13: Age is no proof of anything. We have to prove ourselves sensible, prove ourselves wise, prove ourselves a joy to be around every day of our lives.

October 14: Young people love old people who talk to them — not complain to them, not harp at them, not correct them — just talk to them about the substantial things of life.

October 15: "In youth we learn," Marie von Ebner-Eschenbach wrote. "In age we understand." But only if we work at both.

October 16: Don't be afraid of getting older; but fear like the plague the possibility of losing the lust for life.

October 17: What we ourselves do not nurture in life we will never have. I am the only one who can really make me happy.

October 18: Don't mourn your youth. It's only function is to make "now" a wise and holy, happy and contented place to be.

October 19: Invite an older person out today and ask that person one question: what is the most important thing you ever learned in life and how did you learn it? Then just sit back and listen. You will have the opportunity to learn what no books, no manual, no MBA will ever teach you.

October 20: Our old Sister Leocadia used to say, "You don't have to be crazy to live here, but it sure helps." I know wisdom when I hear it.

October 21: When you're young, you think no one understands you. When you're old, you know it's true. The only difference is that when you're older, you also don't care anymore.

October 22: Old age is that period of life in which we stop striving and start living. The only problem is that it takes so long to get there.

October 23: The aging process is like looking in one of those telescopes on the edge of a public lookout. You look back on all the crises of your life through the lens of time and experience and you're surprised at how small they look. That's called perspective.

October 24: Don't worry about your old age. Simply do something interesting now besides work — like painting or traveling or fishing or reading — and it will be the richest part of your life.

October 25: Kids say, "Never trust anyone over thirty." Senior citizens say, "Anything less than fifty-two and you're not playing with a full deck." They both have a point.

October 26: Life consists of losing some things and gaining others, period after period after period. No single stage of life has it all. That's what is beautiful about it. We all need one another for something — all our lives.

October 27: Don't think of retirement as the end of life. It is simply society's way of giving us permission to live the way we've always wanted to live. Don't apologize for it. You earned it; enjoy it.

October 28:   How to get old may be one of the greatest things we ever get to teach the generation after us.

October 29:   People don't get sweeter, kinder, meaner, fussier, crabbier, more demanding, or less bright just because they're getting older. Whatever we are now we will be then — squared, cubed, multiplied, and in spades. So if you're worried about how loved you'll be when you get old, do something about it now.

October 30:   Take someone half your age to lunch. Ask them to tell you the three values they would like to live by for the rest of their lives and what it is that has led them to that decision. You may well learn what it is that is still to be developed in your own life — if you are to live into the future well.

October 31:   We spend the first part of life accumulating. The second half of life we spend learning how to let go. It is honestly difficult to know which is really the most exciting, the best of the two. There is such a relief that comes with putting down all the burdens. "Those who have cattle have care," the Africans say.

NOVEMBER

PSALM 145

You, O God,
are kind and full
of compassion,
slow to anger,
abounding in love.
You are good to all,
compassionate to all
your creatures.

We talk a lot about the justice of God and the mercy of God. Mercy we ask of a God who is judge. Justice we ask from a God who is righteous. But we may be missing something. The psalmist, unlike us, talks a great deal about the compassion of God, the notion that God is a God who sees our stumbling, suffering lives and suffers our afflictions with us. God, to the psalmist, is a God who feels our feelings and commiserates with them, understands them, knows how they affect us and stands by while we work them through.

God is a father who rocks us through our struggles, a mother who carries us beyond our pain, despite our sense of isolation.

It is for these things we must learn to be thankful. Many people are forgiving. A few are just. But compassionate people are rarer still. The people who simply stand by when we hurt — not trying to talk us out of it, not trying to convince us we're wrong, not demanding that we pretend to be something else — are rare.

It is compassion that supports us in our darkest times, it is compassion for which we are most grateful in life, and it is compassion that we ourselves must develop if we are ever to be worth anything to anyone at all — besides ourselves.

November 1: Thomas Fuller wrote, "There is no coming to heaven with dry eyes." The ability to suffer is what breaks open the human heart to the pain of the world. Until I have known suffering myself, how shall I ever understand anyone else's?

November 2: It is so easy to give charity — a dollar here, a turkey there — but it is of another order entirely to be able to give compassion as well. Compassion is more than kindness. Compassion is that quality of soul that enables me to feel what I cannot possibly understand: the AIDS patient's need for love, the unemployed person's need for dignity, the need of the elderly for respect.

November 3: It's not difficult to give thanks for what we call the good things of our lives — the home, the security, the job, the family. But have you ever considered the value of giving thanks for things that made life very difficult for us — the job we didn't get, the parent we didn't have, the health we lost? Try this prayer today, "Whatever has been, has been best for me; and for that I am always grateful."

November 4: List fifty things that are wrong in your life — right now. List them. Keep thinking. That's right — call it silly if you must. But when you finish the list you'll know that it is no sillier to count such worthless things than it is to walk around complaining about that kind of meaningless nonsense.

November 5: Thomas à Kempis, considered one of the more rigorous of the world's spiritual directors, wrote, "Be assured that if you knew all, you would pardon all." There are circumstances behind every circumstance. Circumstances may not always justify what a person does, but they always explain it, make it reasonable, make it understandable. We may not know them, but they are always there. Believe that and you will never be closed to anybody in the world.

November 6: The deadliest burden in life has got to be the knowledge that nobody understands me and nobody cares. That's why the person who is compassionate saves lives.

November 7: Name the one person you know you can always talk to about anything at any time and know you will be received without correction, evaluation, or reproof. You are a very blessed person.

November 8: George Eliot had it right when she said, "We want people to feel with us more than to act for us." Most people don't want us to "fix" things for them, in other words. They want people to listen to things, to understand things, to help us sort things out for ourselves. Try it and watch all the people who had stopped coming to you for the advice they didn't want come back for the compassion they need more than they needed advice.

November 9: "One can never pay in gratitude," Anne Morrow Lindbergh wrote. "One can only pay in-kind somewhere else in life." We don't give things to people because they need them. We give things to people because someone, somewhere gave to us — and now it's our turn. Thanksgiving, you see, is a game of "Pass-it-on."

November 10: To be a presence of perpetual thanksgiving may be the ultimate goal of life. The thankful person is the one for whom life is simply one long exercise in the sacred.

November 11: Have you ever been around someone who complains all the time? How long did you stay with that person? That's what I thought; so take a lesson. Write down all the things you complained to someone about today. Tomorrow, try for one less complaint and one more friend.

November 12: Today, don't correct anyone. Just listen. Most of all, listen for the things people do not say. Then, respond to those things: "You sound excited." "You seem happy about that." "You look irritated." The message under the words is what people really want to talk about. Listen compassionately.

November 13: Thanksgiving is a feast that was instituted only after the pilgrims had withstood great sacrifice and difficult living. It was not a feast of baubles; it was a recognition of the glory of survival. What have you survived this year that is worth your gratitude? Forget all the fixtures and gadgets and extras in which you're steeped. Give thanks for the real riches of life, the things that make you what you are down deep.

November 14: When you feel besieged on all sides, give thanks for the one thing in life that makes you feel good even under pressure: good music, that special warm hand, the pet that never moves from your side, the child who makes life worth living. After all, it isn't what burdens us, it's what saves us in hard times that ought to be at the center of our hearts.

November 15: Compassion is not nodding "yes, yes" behind the daily paper while someone stands in front of us trying to have their heart heard.

November 16: The difficulty faced by the caretakers of the world — pastoral ministers, counselors, parents — does not lie in having to talk to one person after another. It is being able to summon the energy and the interest to compassionate with them — one after the other — all of them facing the same kinds of situations, all dealing with the same kinds of pain, all staggering under the same kinds of losses. That takes effort. Compassion pulls suffering out of the sufferer and love out of the listener.

November 17: Don't be afraid to cry for yourself as well as others. How else will you ever come to realize what tears mean?

November 18: Thanks to suffering we join the human race.

November 19: Institutions give services; only a person can give compassion. That's why we hate answering machines and electronic mail messages. We want to know that we're in this thing with more than a machine to comfort us. We want people to respond humanly to our humanness.

November 20: Thankfulness is not an exercise; it is a state of mind that makes life an adventure, guarantees love even on bad days, and, in the long run, reduces life stress. Being thankful, however, does not imply that we should tell ourselves that we're grateful for things that eat away at our lives and destroy the very fiber of our souls. If there is a nail in your shoe, take it out. Walking around saying that you're thankful for it is a disease of its own.

November 21: "Thaw with her gentle persuasion is more powerful than Thor with his hammer," Ralph Waldo Emerson wrote. Just once, try to understand the person at whom you are angry instead of evaluating that person. Be "slow to anger" like God. That's compassion. It will change your own life.

November 22: God gives every one of us what we need to bear our burdens and survive our blessings, whether we deserve it or not. Name one burden you wish you could have put down but did not and one blessing that was almost more than you could handle but came to manage well. What saved you in each case? Be thankful for that.

November 23: Emma Goldman wrote, "The motto should not be: forgive one another; rather, understand one another." In fact, I'm not sure we can ever forgive what we do not come to understand.

November 24: Strange, isn't it? We expect that God will show us mercy; but, too often, we show so little ourselves. We believe fiercely in capital punishment; we tolerate the thought of nuclear war; we suspect whatever is unlike ourselves. If heaven is based on the same punitive, violent, and segregating principles, we are all in trouble.

November 25: "Saving lives is not a top priority in the halls of power," Myriam Miedzian wrote. "Being compassionate and concerned about human life can cause a man to lose his job. It can cause a woman not to get the job to begin with."

November 26: The psalmist describes what every human being needs in life: an environment that is kind to a fault, slow to anger, and aware of our suffering. It seems so simple. So where do you suppose it goes wrong? With what kind of person are you harsh when you could be kind? Over what things do you show anger and why? What kind of suffering are you most inclined to ignore? Know those things and you will know why you fail in compassion when you do.

November 27: It's not hard to be compassionate. Just recall the moment in life that embarrassed you most and remember the person who was kind to you in that shameful moment. Now, be like that person to someone else.

November 28: Thanksgiving is almost the hardest season of the year. Admit it: it is so difficult to be really thankful for the things we take for granted. Thankfulness is a virtue to be cultivated — and it does not come easily to some.

November 29: If you want to be a thankful person, give away something you really like — and then thank God that you don't have to get rid of everything else, too.

November 30: Anytime we needed help in the dark places of life, someone came to help us through, right? They're called angels. How do we know? Easy. Our God is a compassionate God.

DECEMBER

PSALM 89

The heavens declare
your wonders;
the assembly
of your holy ones
praises you.
Who can compare with you,
O God?
Who is like you?

*I*n a society full of violence, plagued by poverty, un-accustomed to being poor, and full of expectations unmet, praise has become a foreign subject. We work for what we get, we think. We struggle for what we become, we argue. We make our own way through life, we imagine. What a poor approach to life. It puts the burden for appreciation on the attainment of our unlimited, and perhaps even warped, aspirations instead of attuning us to the beauties already around us, brought there without our efforts, growing there without our permission. Praise is the ability to see everything — not simply what we want to see or expect to see. That's why Christmas is such a surprise. It is the feast of praise where we would never expect to find it.

December 1: Praise is not for sissies. In fact, some people find the whole idea of prayers of praise very hard to take. After all, life is made up of tough stuff, not marshmallow, and praise too often sounds like marshmallow. But it's not. Praise is faith made conscious. And that takes strength.

December 2: We used to have a sister in the community whose favorite saying was, "Watch how you word your prayers because whatever you're praying for you're going to get." So, if she's right — and I have a sneaking suspicion that she is — then if you pray for faith, you can be sure of darkness, and if you pray for hope, you can be sure of despair. Otherwise, there is no need for either faith or hope. Get it? In that case, though, praise is not simply about gifts we see. Praise requires that we give thanks for things, the goodness of which we do not see but must learn to trust.

December 3: It is not hard to see God in the magnificent. What is holy is that we are finally able to see God in the mundane.

December 4: We talk a lot about the need to praise God. I think it is equally necessary to praise people in whom we see the gifts of God. When we praise people we encourage them to go on doing good. Praise someone today—warmly, openly, sincerely, and watch the good things of God multiply before your very eyes.

December 5: We talk about the need to praise God, but we find it hard to accept praise ourselves. That's a shame because what people are really praising when they praise us is God's work in us. Be quiet and take it. For God's sake.

December 6: The question is not, Do you praise God? The question is, What God do you praise? Mohandas Gandhi wrote, "I consider myself a Hindu, Christian, Moslem, Jew, Buddhist and Confucian." Is your God a Christian God? Or simply God? And what does that mean to you?

December 7: "Ritual is the way we carry the presence of the sacred," Christina Baldwin wrote. "Ritual is the spark that must not go out." When we cease to praise God in formal, conscious ways, we cease to cultivate the divine in ourselves. Then we are only half the human being that we are meant to be.

December 8: Religion and spirituality are not the same thing. Religion is a vehicle for spirituality that we too often substitute for the thing itself.

December 9: Prayers of praise should lead to a sense of praise that makes every aspect of life something to be embraced with confidence even when it cannot be embraced with joy.

December 10: A commitment to praise is what reminds us that we are not our own gods.

December 11: Sometimes it's more enlightening to think about what happens to a life devoid of a sense of praise than it is to think about praise itself. When we stop praising God, we start complaining about everything else.

December 12: Why was Jesus born in a stable? Simple: to show us that there is nothing in life that is totally without some good in it.

December 13: Constant complaint sours life not only for ourselves, but for everyone around us as well.

December 14: Name three things that you were consciously thankful for this week. Two? One? Think about it: are you selling life short?

December 15: One reason that we lose a sense of praise is because we live life too much in the same rut, the all too familiar routine, the patterns that smother. Do something different this week. I know you think you don't have time, you're too tired, it's too late to plan something. Forget the excuses. The hole you're in you've dug yourself. Crawl out of it, get an airing, go someplace new. Do something. And praise will rise in your heart like leaven in bread.

December 16: It's easy to praise spring, summer, and fall, but what is there about winter that you recognize as a gift from God? That's praise.

December 17: We love to praise the ineffable, the mysterious, the other-worldly manifestations of God. It's so simple to praise the God we do not see. The real presence of the sacred in life, however, comes when we begin to recognize God in what we do see. Where did God appear to you this week? Think.

December 18: God is not simply to be praised when things go the way we want them to go. God is to be praised when life betrays our best hopes and we survive it anyway.

December 19: Nature praises God, the psalmist implies, by simply being what it is meant to be. We need to do the same. "We are not human beings trying to be spiritual," Jacquelyn Small writes. "We are spiritual beings trying to be human." When we are the most humane humans we can possibly be, God will be fully praised. Not until.

December 20: God is a not a series of fairy tales. God is the supreme question of life. When we stop wondering about God, we stop praising. Asking questions is not a sign of faithlessness. It is the sign of an adult spirituality. God is bigger than anything we have been told.

December 21: Reverence for the earth is a sign of praise. To praise the Creator it is necessary to care for the creation.

December 22: The most wonderful thing that can happen in life is to have something before which we simply stand in awe — a person, a scientific process, a universe of unknown dimensions. Whatever we see that is bigger than ourselves gives us the opportunity to feel the greatness of God.

December 23: When we learn to live at peace with nature, we shall become again people of praise. It is something we failed to learn from Native Americans when we took their land. Now our streams, our food products, and our children are paying the price for our lack of it.

December 24: Praise does not require submission. Praise requires awareness. It elevates the human spirit because it tells us who we are and of what we are made.

December 25: The God we praise sent Jesus as an infant. Now what can we possibly make of that unless it is that God is where we are not looking? Maybe that's why praise comes so hard for us.

December 26: When we begin to recognize the spark of the divine in nature we shall again begin to recognize it in ourselves.

December 27: For one minute put down everything you are disturbed about, concerned about, upset about, worried about and say a prayer of praise for all those good things you take for granted but forget in the midst of your agitations.

December 28: Name the three things for which you give God the greatest praise at this stage of your life. Are you more or less spiritual as a result of them?

December 29: The Latin proverb teaches: God will be present, whether asked or not. The secret of a life of praise is to discover the presence of God where, before, you may have missed it.

December 30: "When you bow deeply to the universe, it bows back. When you call out the name of God, it echoes inside you," Morihei Veshiba said. Which is simply another way of saying that we get out of life what we put into it.

December 31: Put praise back into your life and find what you have been missing — happiness.

Welcome to...

The Monastic Way

by Joan D. Chittister, OSB

If you are a seeker of the sacred...
If spirituality is an important part of your life...
If you would like a daily companion along the way...

Subscribe to...

The Monastic Way

This monthly, single-page publication with daily reflections by one of today's most inspiring religious writers and speakers is ideal for:

- Personal daily reflection
- Homily starters
- Opening prayers for classes, meetings, group gatherings
- Faith sharing

$15 per year includes postage; add $3 for overseas mailing.

Send to *Benetvision,* 355 E. Ninth St., Erie, PA 16503 or call (814) 459-5994. Fax: (814) 459-8066

Quantity discounts available upon request.

ORDER FORM for The Monastic Way
Use this order form for your personal subscription or gift subscriptions.

Name of recipient _____

Address _____

City _____ State _____ ZIP_____

Phone (_____)_____

If gift, name of sender _____

☐ $15 is enclosed for each subscription ($12 subscription + $3 postage). (Please add an extra $3.00 for overseas mailing.)

☐ Quantity discounts are available upon request.

Mail to: *Benetvision,* 355 East Ninth St., Erie, PA 16503-1107
Phone (814) 459-5994   Fax (814) 459-8066